FIRE SERVICE
FIELD TRAINING PROGRAM

FIRE SERVICE

FIELD TRAINING PROGRAM

Mentoring and Training the New Firefighter

Steven Mitchell

Authored and published by Steven P. Mitchell in cooperation with Vistane Group LLC (www.vistanegroup.com) .

Book ISBN: 9798386211929

Forward

This manual is a great road map to developing and implementing an effective Fire Service Field Training Program. Such a program will aid a Fire Department in continuing the post academy training for a new firefighter recruit. The process can also be successfully used for departments that do not use an academy for initial training.

This manual will explain the purpose and role of the program within the Fire Department. It briefly touches on communication concepts that are important to success. The manual explains adult learning principles, proper approaches to training and putting together a training plan.

The FSFTP Manual details using the Coach-Pupil teaching concepts to train firefighters on-the-job. The Program gives the Instructor examples of how to handle recruit decision errors and the evaluation process.

The Manual will tie it all together with discussion on step-by-step development of the FSFTP program, program binders and the roles of the various ranks and positions within the Fire Department to ensure an effective program.

Using this FSFTP Manual as a Guide, you will be able to develop and implement an improved recruit training program.

Table of Contents

Chapter 1 – Introduction

"Tell me and I forget, teach me and I may remember, involve me and I learn,"
Benjamin Franklin

Learning Objectives

- The reader will be able to -
- Identify the training level of a Fire Service Training Program Developer.
- Identify the training level of a Fire Service Training Instructor/Mentor/Coach.
- Identify how the Fire Service Training Program can be used at levels other than the new firefighter.

Being a firefighter comes with a certain degree of risk. That risk is reduced and somewhat controlled through training, building experience and confidence. A new recruit firefighter may not have the experience yet and must rely on the training provided. Some of that training will come on-the-job. It is up to the Fire Department to make sure the recruit has the training needed to be safe and successful.

Whether you are a volunteer, paid-on-call, combination, or full-time fire department you likely rely on some type of traditional on-the-job training program to help teach new recruits. Some of these programs may be formal, most are typically informal in the fact they do not have a structured program with documentation and proper evaluation. The Fire Service Field Training Program has been developed in order to assist your department develop and successfully implement a standardized on-the-job training program. Such a program provides a high degree of professionalism and quality performance, but also reduces the risk of injuries, property damage, improper behavior, and department embarrassment.

It does not really matter what you name the formal role, such as a Fire Service Field Training Instructor, Mentor or Coach the end goal and result are the same. For the sake of this book, we will call the role an **FSFTI**. The personnel that develop your program within your department should be Certified Fire Instructor II or receive the assistance of an Instructor II or Consultant utilizing information in this program. It is strongly recommended that the personnel that are chosen as FSFTI/Mentor/Coach are Certified Fire Instructor I or above plus having studied the <u>Fire Service Field Training Program</u>.

This book provides a good background of information that is relevant to building a positive and effective Field Training Program. It is not a specific certification program but provides the Fire Service Instructor with the information needed to build an effective in-house training program. It also prepares the FSFTI for the role.

While this program is written focused on new recruits, it can be used for the development of all fire department roles and levels. For example, let us consider an Engine Company utilizing a Field Training Program at all levels. Position 4 is a new recruit fresh out of the academy. This is your student for the FSFTI. Position 3 is a 3–5-year Firefighter, this is your formal FSFTI working with the new recruit. The Engineer/Driver/Operator is a 9-year firefighter with 2.5 years of experience as the Driver. This is your FSFTI for the 3 – 5 year firefighter that aspires for the next level. The Lieutenant is a 12-year veteran firefighter with 2 years in his role, and now becomes the FSFTI for the Driver that aspires to become a Lieutenant. Using the same framework for all levels, this is the ultimate succession planning scenario for your department. Eventually the recruit becomes the new FSFTI.

Chapter 2 – Purpose and Role of the Fire Service Field Training Program

---

The Purpose of the Fire Service Field Training Program is to provide a structure that aids in the ability to safely move a recruit from the basic training academy to performing as a quality and effective firefighter and team member.

Learning Objectives

- The reader will be able to -
- Identify and define the four primary goals of the Fire Service Field Training Program.
- Identify and define key advantages of the Fire Service Field Training Program.
- List the attributes of a Fire Service Field Training Instructor/Mentor/Coach.
- Learn the process of developing a Fire Service Field Training Program Policy.

Basic Goals of a Supervised Field Training Program

The first goal of the Fire Service Field Training Program is to provide a structured and standardized learning experience in preparation for an assignment as a non-probationary firefighter. Utilizing a structured program with learning objectives ensures that the teaching and mentoring of new recruits throughout the department is consistent. While different instructors may have some of their own "tricks of the trade," stressing the standardized learning objectives will develop an organization that is efficient, safe, and consistent across the board.

The second goal of the Program is to transfer classroom and academy training to the real situations and challenges of a firefighter's daily activities. Once the academy is completed, it is time to take that new knowledge and concepts and apply it to actual working conditions.

The third goal of the Program is to provide a mentor, a guide, a role model in the form of a Firefighter Fire Service Field Training Instructor. The new recruit will not only be learning the Knowledge, Skills, Abilities (KSAs) of being a firefighter, but also that of fire station etiquette. The recruit will be able to look to the FSFTI for guidance on what is and is not acceptable.

The last goal on our list is to provide a consistent and documented evaluation of recruit performance. While this is important in the retention vs. termination decision process, it can also validate selection procedures and training methods used by the department. Documentation is very important to defend against any false liability or human resource related claims. As the end of the probationary period nears, the department leadership can determine the readiness of the recruit.

Key Advantages of the Field Training Program

Being provided a mentor or Field Training Instructor along with a structured training program will help the new recruit feel welcome in the fire station team environment and more comfortable in the new role. Increasing the possibility of higher quality, better trained and reliable personnel benefit the fire department by making it more effective and efficient. The ultimate benefit is then realized by the community through the quality of service that is provided.

Roles and Attributes of the Fire Service Field Training Program Instructor

- Coach/Teacher
- Facilitator/Information Source
- Role Model
- Counselor
- Performance Evaluator

Fire Service Field Training Program Keys

- Management and Supervisor Support
- FSFTI/Mentor properly selected and trained
- Consider FSFTI/Mentor compensation
- Proper Documentation
- Sufficient time for the proper on the job training
- FSFTI/Mentor connection with the Fire Academy
- Assignment rotations
- Written performance evaluation guidelines

In order for the Fire Service Field Training Program to be successful it will require full buy in and support at all levels. The roles of the Company Officer and the FSFTI supervising the training of the recruit must be clear and understood. In order to implement the program, it is recommended that a policy statement or SOG be developed to set forth the aspects of the program and clarify roles. This should include a process of selection of the FSFTI.

The Policy or SOG will provide details of providing time for the FSFTI to have with the recruit, and how documentation and written performance evaluations will take place. The actual performance objectives, check sheets and evaluation procedures will be located in the FSFTP Training Plan.

Fire Service Field Training Program Policy/SOG

- Define the program. Create the Mission and Vision of the Program.
- Explain role of the program within the overall training program and Mission/Vision of the Department.
- Stress the support required at all levels.
- List FSFTI requirements and selection process.
- Consider a job description for the FSFTI.
- Describe, but do not include, the FSFTP Training Plan.
- Describe time elements.
- List required documentation and written evaluations.

Company
Officer

FSFTI   Recruit

- The Policy must explain the professional and accountability relationship between the Recruit, FSFTI and Company Officer. It should also explain formal reporting lines of the FSFTI for recruit documentation and evaluation. The FSFTI and Company Officer must work together to achieve the program goals.

Chapter 3 – Communication Skills for the FSFTI

Being a member of the Fire Service Field Training Program requires the ability to communicate effectively with superiors as well as communicate with the recruit as a coach.

Learning Objectives

- The reader will be able to -
- Define communication.
- List and define the communication components.
- List the elements of Instructor/Pupil communication in a Fire Service setting.
- Learn and discuss barriers to communication.
- Learn and discuss the various forms of non-verbal communication.

The effectiveness of the Fire Service Field Training Program will depend on the communication skills of all of those involved. Written communication skills will be on demand for the proper documentation and performance evaluation of the recruit firefighter. Effective verbal communication skills are a vital part of the coaching process. The department should welcome and invite any chance to have personnel attend classes or workshops that can improve both written and verbal communication skills. There are also many books and periodicals available to assist in improvement of these skills.

Communication is the means of transferring knowledge. Through effective communication you have the ability to show confidence and increase the level of confidence in the receiver. It is important that the FSFTI have self-awareness during discussions with a recruit. Positive communication is imperative to the department Mission as a whole. Even during performance evaluation and counseling the communication should always lean toward a positive end. Negative tones can stay with and be reflected from the recruit for the duration of a career.

Communication Components

There are basically three parts of sending a message verbally. The most obvious is the verbal or what you are going to say, the actual words. However, when decoding a receiver only places about 7% of the processing on the words. 38% of the processing is on how the message was said, the voice inflections. The largest part of the processing is placed on the non-verbal expressions and demeanor of the sender at 55%.

The reception of the message includes listening, interpreting, and internalizing. The FSFTI will have gauge the listening skills of the recruit over a period of time. Such skills are hopefully at a high level coming out of the academy. Interpreting and internalizing a spoken message by the receiver will go through many filters, experiences and biases the receiver has acquired over a lifetime. For example, some type of perceived negative word or phrase will ramp up the focus by the receiver. Not handled properly it can place the receiver on guard the remainder of the conversation. The receiver at that point may start decoding the message with a different perspective.

Communication from a formal FSFTI to a recruit must be in a form to build trust and make the recruit feel comfortable. However, when speaking to the recruit the FSFTI is speaking for the fire department (employer) and not as an individual.

The communication must be

- Legal
- Ethical
- Professional
- Uphold integrity of the Department, Program, and the FSFTI/Mentor
- Confident
- Accurate
- Truthful
- Within employer standards and policy

Perception and Barriers Effect on Communications

During communication, the perception of the receiver will define the reality of the communicated message. Perception can also affect how the sender communicates the message. It is possible that two people can interpret the same message different ways. Due to perception, both can actually be right. As mentioned earlier, there are several factors that go into how a message is perceived. These may include:

- Personal experience
- Values
- Personal Filters
- Selective listening
- Trigger words

For the FSFTI, having self-awareness and gradually learning the recruit will be important in making sure the proper learning message is conveyed and learned. Learn and avoid potential perception blocks such as selective perception, self-fulfilling prophecy, stereotyping and halo-horns affects. You also need to understand where your student is in the Hierarchy of Needs in order to help understand the human behavior. As a reminder these are:

- Physical Needs
- Security Needs
- Affection and Affiliation
- Esteem
- Self-Actualization

During the communication process, there may also be some barriers or limitations in the communication process, especially in the on-the job situation. These may include:

- Situational stress
- Atmosphere
- Weather, Temperature
- Noise
- Fatigue
- Illness
- Mental
- Bias
- Impatient
- Preoccupied
- Misuse or misunderstanding of words

Non-Verbal Communication

- Eye Contact
  - Looking to right using imagination or visual thinker
  - Looking to the left recalling a specific memory
  - Inability to make eye contact boredom, deceit, shy or uncomfortable
  - Looking down may be disinterested

- Gestures/Body Language
  - Crossed arms may be closed off or could be comfortable or cold. Watch facial expressions also.
- Posture/Presence
  - Feet pointed forward, good feeling about you
- Facial expressions
  - Is a smile genuine, nervous, sarcastic, or fake
  - Nodding means interest
  - Tight lips, annoyed
  - Relaxed mouth, interested or positive
- Use of Objects
  - Clicking a pen
  - Tapping a Pencil
- Physical distancing
- Appearance

The FSFTI should learn to use body language that demonstrates confidence and provides comfort to the recruit. It is also necessary to learn over time the non-verbal cues from the recruit. Non-Verbal communication can be a complex subject of study. Going into great depth on non-verbal communication is outside the scope of this book. It is recommended that the FSFTI seek out specific communication related education and training such as online training and workshops.

Chapter 4 – Adult Learning Principles

Understanding the Principles of Adult Learning will help the Fire Service Field Training Instructor/Mentor be effective and successful.

Learning Objectives

- The reader will be able to -
- List and understand the Adult Learning Principles.
- List and define the Laws of Learning.
- List and define five methods of learning.
- List various characteristics of adult learning.
- List and discuss three Learning Domains.

Learning is an observable, sustained change in behavior and/or performance. If the behavior or performance is not both observable and sustained, then effective learning has not taken place.

Adult Learning Principles

- All human beings can learn.
- The person must be motivated to learn.
- Learning is an active process.
- Those that are learning will need guidance and feedback.
- The proper materials must be provided for learning to occur.
- Time must be provided to practice skills.
- Training methods should be varied during the learning process.

- Correct behavior must be immediately reinforced and repeated.
- Written standards of performance should be set for the learner.

Laws of Learning

Edward Lee Thorndike (1874 – 1949) was a psychologist and professor that researched the science of the learning process and discovered and explained the Laws of Learning.

- *Law of Readiness* is the theory that a person can learn best when both physically and mentally prepared to learn. The FSFTI needs to know that the student/recruit needs are being met and that any barriers to learning have been eliminated or overcome. In order for the recruit/student to be ready to learn the FSFTI must motivate for learning, build rapport, and gain attention.
- *Law of Exercise* refers to the theory that repeated items and tasks are remembered the best if the repetition is meaningful.
- *Law of Effect* shows that learning is much stronger and more effective when it is accompanied by some type of feeling of satisfaction or reward.
- *Law of Association is* also discussed above under Methods of Learning. The mind will try to compare learning something new with something that is already known or has been experienced. In some cases, an FSFTI may even want to help a student/recruit make a connection in order to help the learning process. Use a personal story of using the task being learned in a real case scenario.
- *Law of Intensity* while not necessarily rewarding or satisfying causes learning to occur because it is real and exciting. A vivid learning experience will be remembered much better than one that is boring.
- *Law of Recency* refers to the fact that the last thing learned will be the thing remembered the best. This is why a review of knowledge or skill occurs before a testing process.

- Note: Something you are trying to teach will soon be forgotten if the learning is not reinforced.

Methods of Learning

Imitation is the ability of the student to observe a model and then pattern their behavior after that model. This is a typical coach-pupil method for learning a new skill. This is active teaching and learning through listening, direct observation, and interaction.

Insight is when a student suddenly gets it. It typically happens when you least expect it. This may occur during a lesson, or possibly while the student is practicing or studying on their own.

Association and transfer are when a student begins to build upon past experience or what they may already know. This could be from a previous experience or may be from what was learned in the recruit academy. As the FSFTI you need to understand that this could also lead to errors or improper methods that may need to be corrected.

Conditioning refers to a task or learning subject that the student responds to automatically. They learn it very quickly.

Trial and success are a common method for hands on tasks. The student continues to try something until they finally gain success, and then continue to practice gaining sustained performance. Fire service knots would be a very good example.

Characteristics of Adult Learning

- Adults are typically highly motivated to learn.
- Adults have more life experiences than that of children.

- People may likely reject something that is contrary to what they believed in the past. Adults have the need to validate the information based on their own beliefs and experiences.
- Adults decide for themselves what is important to learn.
- An adult could lack self-confidence in ability to learn.
- Adults expect what they learn to be useful immediately.
- An adult may have fixed viewpoints.
- Adults have more roles and responsibilities that compete for time.
- Adults tend to be more different than each other compared to children.
- Adults want to know what they are doing.
- Climate for learning must be adult related.
- Learning can be problem centered.
- Adults will want to set their own pace.
- Learning for adults can be more positive when the student participates in the learning process and setting goals.

There is a point in adult learning where the learning levels may plateau, and the student/recruit will stop learning. This may be caused by barriers to learning such as boredom, fatigue, information, or task too difficult, and/or simply too much information too fast. This is when it is time to break the tension with breaks or slowing down.

Learning Domains

The Cognitive Domain is the knowledge gained in the learning process. There are six primary levels of cognitive learning we will discuss lowest to highest. Having the ability to recall something at a simple level is known as *Knowledge*. The ability to understand the subject, summarize and even explain it to a point is known as *Comprehension*. Application refers to when a person can use the information, typically in a new setting. *Analysis* is when a person can actually break down the subject into parts and conduct troubleshooting. A person may be able to take several different pieces of information or knowledge and bring them all together to form something new. This is known as *Synthesis*. *Evolution* is the point that the person uses judgement and selection of most qualified information based on specific criteria.

During recruit Field Training, we are initially interested in the recruit using Knowledge from the academy as well as gaining new Knowledge and then the ability to Comprehend and Apply that knowledge in a real work situation.

The <u>Affective Domain</u> refers to the attitude of the person toward the learning and the work environment. There are five primary levels of the Affective Domain. *Receiving* refers to the ability to understand the new information but may still not be quite on board with it. The person may still be processing the information based on the various learning methods. When the adult learner begins to do the task properly when the instructor or supervisor is around, this is known as *Responding*. Doing the task properly when the instructor or supervisor is not around is *Valuing*. *Organizing* in the case of the Affective Domain is when the person starts to get others to do the task correctly. *Characterizing* the information or task is when it becomes natural, it is performed correctly every time without thought.

In the case of Field Training a new recruit, obviously at some point Characterizing would be the ultimate goal. However, understand that the recruit will go through all of the phases over a period of time. It may take longer than the FSFTP period to get all required tasks to this level.

The <u>Psychomotor Domain</u> is the final piece and refers to the actual desired skill or behavior being taught by the instructor based on performance objectives. There are five levels of this domain of learning. We start off with the adult learner simply attempting to repeat the actions as observed known as *Imitation*. When the learner can work through and perform the task while receiving instruction it is referred to as *Manipulation*. *Precision* is when the learner can perform the task exactly as desired. When the learner begins to combine the task with other tasks is known as *Articulation*. Finally, the learner will hopefully get to *Naturalization* where several tasks are performed correctly together and in a proper sequence.

The FSFTI must be patient as the new recruit goes through all of the phases in their own time with Naturalization as the ultimate goal.

It should be understood that different types of knowledge and skills/tasks will likely be at different levels at the end of the formal Field Training Program. The process will continue through experience. For most fire service tasks, the FSFTI will probably have a goal to have the recruit at a level to *comprehend* and *apply* knowledge that is *valuing* and performed with *precision* and *articulated* with other tasks in proper sequence. Remember that learning the performance objectives must be observable and sustained.

Chapter 5 – Approaches to Training

We will look at many of the aspects that will lead to the creation of the Field Training Program. Explain the Instructional System Design (ISD) Model as a framework to develop a training program and instructional materials.

Learning Objectives

- The reader will -
- Learn the elements of the Training Formula and the Training Planning Sequence.
- Learn the ISD Model for the planning of training.
- Discuss the necessity for a needs analysis.
- Define a Job and Task Analysis.

In the Fire Service Field Training Program, it will be expected that the FSFTI will be teaching and coaching from already developed performance objectives and criteria. Such planning will take place before the implementation of the Program. Chapter 6 will also discuss planning more in depth.

Skills Required for Job – Mastered Skills = Required Training

Training Planning Sequence/Training Formula

(R)

- Conduct job analysis
- Conduct task analysis
- Conduct needs assessment
- Review/Select training alternatives

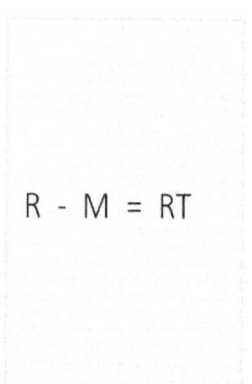

 R: KSAs required for the job

$$R - M = RT$$

 M: KSAs mastered by employee

 RT: Required Training

(M)

- Assess Knowledge and Skills

(RT)

- Sequence Learning Order
- Knowledge before skills
- Develop performance objectives
- Develop Assessment measures
- Determine strategies of instruction
- Develop materials
- Provide Training
- Evaluate Student and Program

ISD Model

Analysis

- Determination of training need
- Defines problems
- Generates information
- Training formula

Design/Development

- Preparation of programs
- Design specifications
- Learning activities determined
- Materials developed
- Lesson plans

Implementation

- Process of putting training programs into operation
- Conduct the training

Evaluation

- Process of interpreting results
- Decision making
- Judgements
- Accountability
- Feedback

Needs Analysis

A needs analysis will identify performance requirements and deficiencies to be followed by the developing, analyzing and identifying solutions. For example, what will the recruit learn in the academy vs. what knowledge and skills does the recruit need to be proficient at to be successful in the field. If you are a department doing all of the teaching in house, then basically you are starting your FSFTP from day one learning.

When using the academy environment, it is important for the FSFTI to have periodic interaction with the academy in order to gain knowledge on exactly what the recruit is learning. Once in house, a training needs analysis could include reviewing academy evaluations, interviewing academy staff, and actually testing and evaluating the recruit.

Job and Task Analysis

A job analysis is a comprehensive look at the duties of a specific position. This is completed through developing and reviewing a detailed list of tasks through observation, interview, and document review. The job analysis should actually be completed before the selection process for the position is developed. This can be handled internally, by the Human Resources Department, or through 3rd party consultant.

Conducted properly, the process may be very complex and time consuming for fire service positions. The job must be broken down into units, then into tasks and finally manageable steps. Considerable data must be acquired and reviewed. A task analysis is the further breaking down of the elements found in the job analysis. In the fire service this could include step by step how to complete a task or use a specific piece of equipment. Luckily this has been completed for many emergencies service-related areas of the fire service in various forms such as IFSTA, Pro Board and IFSAC.

Chapter 6 – Training Plan

A successful Fire Service Field Training Program will have an overall training plan that is broken down into lesson plans.

Learning Objectives

- The reader will be able to -
- List and describe the elements of the Fire Service Field Training Program.
- List, understand and describe the content of a Training Plan.
- Describe how to organize a training plan.
- Learn how to develop performance objectives.
- Discuss the testing and evaluation process.
- List the elements of a Lesson Plan

Program Elements

- Fire Service Field Training Program Department Policy or SOG
  - Policy statement and executive summary.
  - Leadership support statement.
  - Define Program, Set Mission, and Vision of the Program.
  - Define role/position (i.e., FSFTI).
  - Requirements and selection process for FSFTI.
  - Briefly explain establishment of the FSFTP Training Plan.
  - Establish standardized documentation and evaluation procedures.
- FSFTP General Training Plan for Post-Academy Recruits
  - Will you also use it for other positions?
- Performance Objectives
  - FF I and II, EMS, Haz Mat, etc.

- o From Job Description
- o From SOGs
- o In House Duties
- Lesson Plans
  - o Internal Developed
  - o External Developed
- Documentation
  - o Check off sheets breaking down tasks
  - o Written back-up of verbal evaluations
- Written Evaluation
  - o Internal Evaluation Forms
- Performance Improvement Plans

Contents of a Training Plan

- Course Name.
  - o Fire Service Field Training Program for New Recruits
- Course Objectives.
  - o To provide a structured and standardized learning experience in preparation for an assignment as a non-probationary firefighter.
  - o To transfer classroom and academy training to the real situations and challenges of a firefighter's daily activities.
  - o To provide the recruit a mentor, a guide, a role model in the form of a Firefighter Fire Service Field Training Instructor.
  - o To provide a consistent and documented evaluation of recruit performance.
  - o To give the recruit every opportunity to succeed.
- Timeline.
  - o The FSFTP will operate for 36 weeks following the Academy.
- Curriculum
- Suggested Monthly Schedule

- o Note that this is suggested as real world situations will allow for teachable moments.
- o The FSFTI must have the ability to adjust as needed.
- Lesson Plans
  - o Performance Objectives
  - o Procedure
  - o Task Break downs
- Check Lists
  - o Internal Developed
  - o External Developed
- Evaluation Forms
  - o Internal Developed

Organizing Content of Training Plan

1. Simple to Complex
2. General to Specific
3. Known to Unknown
4. Knowledge then Skills

Performance Objectives

The performance objective will describe the behavior or task that must be performed and must have a verb. It will establish a standard or outcome and describe the conditions under which the behavior must be performed.

- Remember to always build safety into all training programs, including on-the-job training.
- Contains an action verb
- Observable
- Measurable

Note: For many fire service tasks the fire department may consider adopting already completed performance objectives and check lists from IFSAC, Pro Board, State, or IFTSA. The department may also write internal performance objectives and will be required to do so for tasks not within the normal FFI and II curriculum or that are department specific.

Elements of a Lesson Plan

- Lesson Title
- Materials and Training Aids needed
- References
- Performance/Learning Objectives
- Instructional Method
- Learning Domains/Methods
- Lesson Outline
- Instructor Notes
- Evaluation Method
- Skill Check Off Sheets (If needed)

Testing/Evaluation

Testing is used to assess knowledge and performance of skills. It provides accountability in that it provides the knowledge and performance at a specific level. In order to test actual learning, once knowledge and skill learning is sustained, it should be tested in real world situations.

A combination of testing works best. Utilize written testing for the cognitive domain and a skills performance test for psychomotor domain. Work attitude is observable and should be documented.

Develop a test plan as part of the overall training plan.

- Identify important content.
- Determine level of learning to be tested at various points throughout the program.
- For skills testing, define exactly what items are needed for the testing.
- If available, utilize already developed testing procedures and questions.

Remember that you simply cannot test on everything for a knowledge test. Select a good cross section of important material.

Chapter 7 - Coach – Pupil Learning Process

The Fire Service Field Training Program will typically utilize the one-on-one training methods of coach-pupil instruction. Set up the recruit to succeed through interactive training.

Learning Objectives

- The reader will -
- Identify the characteristics of the Coach-Pupil Learning Process.
- List important Coach elements.
- Describe an example Coach-Pupil teaching method.

The Coach-Pupil method of instruction is typically interactive one-on-one training used to teach actual physical skills. It utilizes an Explain-Demonstrate-Performance method of instruction.

Characteristics of Coach-Pupil instruction include student centered instruction that is one-on-one requiring the use of most physical senses. Coach-Pupil can be more than one-on-one such as teaching a small group or a fire company.

An advantage of the Coach-Pupil Instruction is that it allows for learning to be more thorough. It allows the FSFTI to build rapport quicker when giving individual attention. The Coach-Pupil method typically allows for immediate or near immediate feedback to include recognition/reward and corrections/modifications of performance behavior.

While there are various arguments for a list of disadvantages of Coach-Pupil Instruction, the only primary one would be that it can be time consuming. Time management is very important in the planning process.

Coach Elements

- Review the Performance Objectives.
- Know your student.
- Use a logical learning sequence.
- Be a subject matter expert. Do your own learning.
- Review and prepare from the lesson plan.
- Rehearse and practice.
- Teach it.
- Evaluate the student.
- Evaluate yourself.

Coach-Pupil Instruction of Skills (Teaching)

- Determine student learning readiness.
- Identify and eliminate barriers, challenges, distractions to learning.
- Tell them what they are going to learn.
- Show them what they are going to learn.
- Demonstrate the skill step-by-step.
- Have the student complete the skill while explaining and even showing again.
- Have the student complete the skill.
- Correct errors, repeat.
- When the student completes the task correctly, immediately have them repeat it.
- Tell them what they just learned.
- Evaluate, recognize.

Using Questions Properly

Using and allowing questions is important in Coach-Pupil Instruction. Establish a coaching environment where the recruit/student feels comfortable asking questions. Not only should you not embarrass a recruit, but you should also acknowledge and praise questions. The Coach should also use questions to gain feedback and assess knowledge. Such questions are usually factual or thought provoking. However, from time-to-time opinion or rhetorical questions may be used to provoke thinking and gain feedback.

A Training Aid is basically anything that can aid in the training of a task. In the Fire Service you will be training with the actual tools and equipment used for the job. This may be anything from selecting and using the proper saw to selecting and using the proper toilet brush.

Teaching Opportunity Locations

- Fire Station
- Apparatus Bay
- Training Center
- Outside (Apron, parking lot, lawn, park)
- Local Fixed Facility
- Working incidents
- In the Field (hydrants, pre-planning, inspections, etc.)

Use of On-line Training

Manufacturers and Firefighters have taken the opportunity to utilize on line venues to show off skills and the use of equipment. If you decide you want to use a video to help demonstrate a specific task or the use of a piece of equipment, do so within certain parameters.

The training video must be reviewed and approved by the Training Officer or Developers of the FSFTP. It is important to make sure that the video follows the step-by-step process that has been approved by the Department.

Once approved, DO NOT simply assign the video and the related learning task and then check on it later. That form is not a training aid. Use the following procedure:

- Determine learning readiness.
- Introduce and explain the lesson.
- Watch the video together.
- Break down the video for the recruit as needed.
- Practice the skill.
- Review parts of the video as needed.
- Demonstrate the skill as needed.
- Have the recruit complete the skill or task.
- Once the recruit demonstrates correctly, have them repeat.
- Reward or correct as needed. Teach, Coach but do not critique.

Chapter 8 – Recruit Decisions

The Fire Service Field Training Instructor/Mentor will need to know how to react to recruit decisions, what methods are available and how to use them.

Learning Objectives

- The reader will learn and understand the proper response to recruit (pupil) actions.

The recruit should be permitted to do everything possible on-the-job within the limitations set forth by the FSFTI or Fire Officer provided the end result is positive development of knowledge, skills, attitudes, and behaviors with consideration of possible injury, property damage, reputation of the department, and legality.

Once again set the recruit up to succeed. The recruit should know in advance what correction techniques you will use and when they will be used so they understand if and when a correction occurs in the field. It is important to not allow a mistake or error be repeated as it then becomes learning. A teachable moment can be used when relevance and importance is at its peak.

Real World teachable moments are very valuable in the learning process for the new recruit or any new position.

Override of Recruit Decisions and Actions

Student action, or task accomplishment requires some type of response from the FSFTI. Most of the time this will hopefully be recognition or acknowledgement of correct performance. However, from time-to-time overrides may be necessary. Overt overrides are used in the event of a serious error such as:

- When serious injury or death could occur
- Cause serious embarrassment to the department
- Violation of the law
- Violation of policy, rules, and regulations
- Property damage may occur
- Violation of civil rights

Student Action	FSFTI Action	Later
Minor procedural error	No immediate action	Correct/Retrain
Non-critical error	Subtle Override	Correct/Retrain
Serious error	Overt Override/Step in Turn back over to recruit when possible	Explain/Retrain for desired performance

Chapter 9 – Evaluations

Review of performance according to specific standard criteria utilizing oral and written means to reward positive performance and provide corrective measures to aid in the learning of desired performance behaviors.

Learning Objectives

- The reader will –
- Define Evaluation.
- Define the purpose for evaluation.
- Be able to list and discuss evaluation types.

Merriam-Webster defines critique as "an act of criticizing" and "to examine critically."

Merriam- Webster defines evaluation as "determination of the value, nature, character, or quality of something or someone."

Our definition of evaluation for this program will be "the review of performance according to specific standard criteria utilizing oral and written means to reward positive performance and provide corrective measures to aid in the learning of desired performance behaviors."

The word "critique" has grown negative meanings over the years and places a student on guard when used. We will not use the word critique in our program as the goal is to always set up the environment for the success of the member and the organization.

Purpose of Evaluation

We want members performing at a specific level in order to achieve a successful high-quality organization for those that we serve. Use evaluations with this in mind. Remember, we not only want the recruit to succeed, but to succeed at a high-quality level.

- Improve performance
- Retention/termination
- Standardize Outcomes
- Feedback
- Identify Training Needs/Training Needs Formula
- Later Evaluation of Instructor and Program

Evaluation will be

- Objective
- Flexible
- Comprehensive
- Organized
- Thoughtful
- Specific to performance objectives

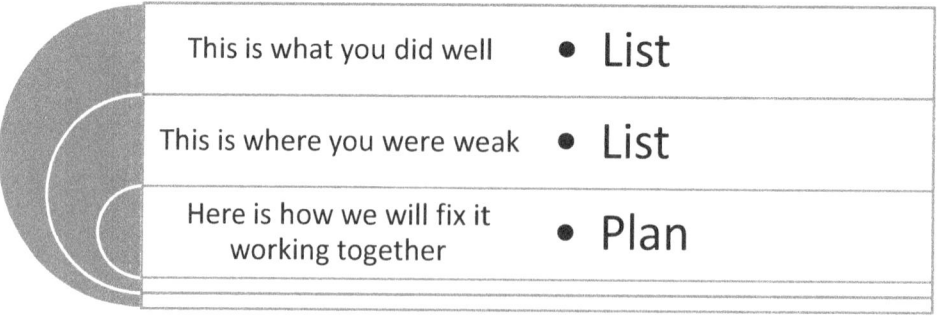

This is what you did well	• List
This is where you were weak	• List
Here is how we will fix it working together	• Plan

Evaluation Types

Oral

> Lesson Feedback
>
> Daily Verbal Evaluation
>
> Documented
>
> Will be the basis for the written rating.

Written

> Written evaluation/appraisal
>
> Task Check Sheets
>
> Monthly
>
> Should not be a surprise, should have already been part of feedback

Oral Review

- Look for the strengths and the weaknesses
- Private setting
- Plan the oral review
- Keep it simple, do not cover too much
- Provide positive guidance
- What needs to be corrected, how is it going to be corrected
- In this order: Reward positive or strength, explain weakness or what needs to be corrected and how it will be corrected, end with positive summary and goals.

You can start an oral review with open ended questions.

"You had your first full code today; how do you think that went?"

"How do you think that extrication went this morning? Any problems with the tools?"

For Oral Feedback have a conversation, not a one-sided critique. Get them talking through open ended questions and then go into the review as part of the conversation. Talk about the good and talk about what needs improvement. Recognize the positive. Give tips and even plan a follow-up training session while it is fresh.

Performance Improvement Plans

The development of a written Performance Improvement Plan may be needed if typical oral reviews and written evaluations are not showing improvement in certain areas or a specific task. The written plan will detail the Performance Requirement, The Problem or Deficiency, The Goal, The Action Plan to Reach the Goal, The Support that will be required and offered, The Standards or Metrics to include a timeline, and the Consequences if the Performance is not satisfactory.

Decision Making

The documentation of oral feedback, written evaluations and Performance Improvement Plans are very important in the employee decision making process to answer the questions:

"Is the member progressing at a positive rate?"

"Is the member having learning issues?"

"Is the member salvageable as a future team member?"

Chapter 10 – Summary

Learning Objectives

- The reader will list in order the elements to build a Fire Service Field Training Program.

Building a Fire Service Field Training Program Step by Step

1. Fire Department Leadership commits to the use of a FSFTP.
2. Develop the Mission and Vision of the FSFTP. (See the book <u>Vision Marksmanship for Fire and EMS Services</u>)
3. Conduct analysis of the training need. (Chapter 5)
4. Develop the Fire Department FSFTP Policy or SOG. (Chapter 6)
5. Determine who will develop the program. (Chapter 1)
6. Train and educate the FSFTP developers with this book.
7. Develop the FSFTP Training Plan. (Chapter 6)
8. Incorporate the Learning Domains, Learning Type and Methods to be used properly throughout the program. (Chapter 4)
9. Develop Lesson Plans and skill check off sheets. (Chapter 6)
10. Develop testing and evaluation methods.
11. Select the FSFTI. (Department Policy)
12. Train the FSFTI as Instructor I and with this book. (All Chapters)
13. Market the FSFTP to the Fire Department to get buy in at all levels.
14. Implement Program.
15. Stick to the program, evaluate, and make changes as needed.

Fire Service Field Training Program Binder

FSFTP Policy

Training Plan

General Training Schedule

Lesson Plans

Skill Check Off Sheets

Oral Feedback Documentation Forms

Formal Written Evaluation Forms

Formal Written Report

Fire Service Field Training FSFTI Binder
Recruit Specific

Recruit Name/Recruit Academy Summary

Training Plan for Recruit/Recruit Training Goals

Specific Training Schedule

Lesson Plans

Skill Check Off Sheets

Oral Feedback Documentation Forms

Formal Written Evaluation Forms

Formal Written Report

Fire Service Field Training Program Roles and Relationships

The success of the program will depend upon each person involved to know and understand their role and reporting lines in the recruit training. This includes who gets to see the FSFTI feedback and evaluations. This needs to be identified and clarified before the training starts. For example, the role of each of the following should be identified and clarified:

Fire Chief – Retention decision.

Department Training Chief – Overall training requirements; Records retention; Provide Guidance to FSFTI; alter Training Plan as needed; schedules outside training.

Shift Commander – Final Probationary and retention recommendation.

Company Officer – Quarterly and Final Probationary Evaluations.

Fire Service Field Training Instructor – Recruit Training, Routine Oral (Daily) and Written (Monthly) Evaluation; regular oral reports to CO; monthly written reports to CO, SC and TO.

In this scenario, the Department Training Chief, Shift Commander, Company Officer and FSFTI will work closely together to monitor the progress of the recruit. Regular meetings of this group would be recommended along with the evaluations and reports. While the FSFTI will do the day-to-day oral feedback with the recruit, the developers of the program may want to have the monthly formal evaluations with the recruit to include the FSFTI and the Company Officer. However, such meeting must be constructive, so the recruit does not feel being ganged up on with more than one evaluator in the meeting.

Also decide and include in the Policy how the FSFTI will be evaluated.

Chapter 11 – Evaluation of Learning

After each Chapter, take time to answer the relevant questions below in order to help facilitate the learning of Fire Service Field Training Program development and implementation.

Chapter 1

1. What Instructor level should be obtained by a Fire Service Training Program Developer?
2. What Instructor level should be obtained by a Fire Service Training Instructor/Mentor/Coach?
3. Explain how the Fire Service Training Program can be used at levels other than the new firefighter.

Chapter 2

4. List and define the four primary goals of the Fire Service Field Training Program.
5. List and explain key advantages of the Fire Service Field Training Program.
6. List the attributes of a Fire Service Field Training Instructor/Mentor/Coach.
7. Briefly explain the process of developing a Fire Service Field Training Program Policy.

Chapter 3

8. Define communication.
9. List and define the communication components.
10. List the elements of Instructor/Pupil communication in a Fire Service setting.
11. List and explain barriers to communication.
12. List the various forms of non-verbal communication.

Chapter 4

13. List and describe the Adult Learning Principles.
14. List and define the Laws of Learning.
15. List and define five methods of learning.
16. List various characteristics of adult learning.
17. List and discuss three Learning Domains.

Chapter 5

18. List the elements of the Training Formula and the Training Planning Sequence.
19. Explain the necessity for a needs analysis.
20. Define a Job and Task Analysis.

Chapter 6

21. List and describe the elements of the Fire Service Field Training Program.
22. List the content of a Training Plan.
23. Describe how to organize a training plan.
24. Explain how to develop performance objectives.
25. What is the purpose of testing and evaluation?
26. List the elements of a Lesson Plan.

Chapter 7

27. List the characteristics of the Coach-Pupil Learning Process.
28. List important Coach elements.

Chapter 8

29. Explain one response to recruit (pupil) actions.

Chapter 9

30. Define Evaluation.
31. List the evaluation types.

Chapter 10

32. List, in order, the elements to build a Fire Service Field Training Program.

INDEX

About the Author

Chief (ret.) Steven Mitchell is the Managing Member of Vistane Group LLC which operates Vistane Group Consulting and Vistane Group Leadership Coaching. Mitchell has a well-rounded background with experience in both the public and private sectors which includes 37 years of experience in the fire service and ownership of various private sector businesses. With many in leadership roles, he has 16 years of experience as a full-time municipal Fire Chief and also served five years as an elected County Commissioner. Mitchell has Degrees in Business Administration and Fire Service Administration and completed Graduate Study in the areas of Organizational Development and Adult Education. He also has Graduate Certificates in Professional Supervision and Emergency Management. Designated as a Chief Fire Officer (CFO) by the Center for Public Safety Excellence, Mitchell also holds Certified Fire Protection Specialist (CFPS) from the NFPA and is a ten-time recipient of the National Life Safety Achievement Award. He was the 2013 Career Fire Chief of the year for Kentucky awarded by the Kentucky Association of Fire Chiefs and Kentucky League of Cities, as well as many other recognitions. Mitchell is the creator and trademark holder of "Vision Marksmanship," a program used to help organizations achieve desired goals. Vision Marksmanship for Fire and EMS Services is available on Amazon. He has mentored many current and past leaders and assisted organizations achieve success in both the private and public sectors.

www.ingramcontent.com/pod-product-compliance
Lightning Source LLC
Chambersburg PA
CBHW070750220526
45467CB00018B/1804